SABBY the SEA OTTER

A Pup's True Adventure and Triumph

KIM STEINHARDT

Co-author of The Edge: The Pressured Past and Precarious Future of California's Coast

CRAVEN STREET BOOKS

Fresno, CA

In the surf and foam where the deep blue ocean meets the shoreline, there lived a little sea otter named Sabby. He was about the size of a shoe box, not counting his floppy tail. That tail was almost as long as he was.

Sabby was only four weeks old when a great adventure changed his life. This tale is true and must be told so little sea otters everywhere can understand what the world is like, and so we can understand what the world is like for little sea otters everywhere.

It all began early one spring.

Sabby lived with his mom in a small **lagoon** beside the ocean along California's central coast. Colorful birds of all kinds filled the waters. There were **egrets** with snowy feathers, pretty **pelicans** with large beaks, and great blue **herons**.

3

The lagoon was alive with **seals**, **sea lions** and, of course, other **sea otters**.

Lots of silvery **sardines** swam in the waters. Even a small **octopus** or two peeked out from the nearby rocks. **Mussels**, **clams**, and **sea urchins** made their homes on the bottom, along the mud, and in the rocks.

Sabby loved to listen and to watch. He was always amazed by the activity and sounds in the lagoon, with birds calling out, clams squirting on the beach, and sea lions barking noisily at one another all day long.

Sometimes when it was cool, and wisps of fog rolled in, he would just listen to the wind. Other times, when it was very clear and the sun was bright, he would turn up his furry face like other otters and peer into the sky to watch the birds. Every now and then, the shadow of a soaring gull would cross his face and startle him.

Sabby had a good life.

For a little pup like Sabby—baby sea otters are called pups—it takes time to learn how to swim. Sabby wasn't very good at it yet. He was young and had not fully gotten all the tricks his mom had taught him.

Sometimes he zigged when he wanted to zag. Sometimes he just went in little circles when he wanted to go straight. Other times, when he swam against a big **current** of rushing water, he didn't go anywhere at all. But sometimes he got to where he wanted to go.

Sabby had plenty of fun splashing and bouncing, with bubbles all around. So much to do!

Since Sabby was so little, his mom worked hard to take very good care of him. She carefully groomed his fine fur to keep it clean and healthy. She also fed Sabby. Since sea otters dive underwater to find their food, she taught him how to gather clams and crabs and mussels—called shellfish—so he could begin to feed himself.

She showed him how she would pick up a rock from deep underwater with her paws and put it on her chest. While she floated on her back on top of the water, she'd crack open a clam or a mussel against that rock. She gripped the shellfish tightly in her paws, using her claws. Raising her powerful arms, she quickly lifted and banged it down on the rock—*crack! crack! crack!*—until the shell broke open.

Sea otters are voracious. (That's the fancy way to say they eat a lot.)

Mussels were definitely his favorite. He could smell them, and he always wanted to taste them. Imagine sharing a gooey, orange mussel!

You could see Sabby loved his mom. She stayed by his side tirelessly to protect him and teach him the ways of the ocean.

Whenever it came time to go from here to there in the ocean or the lagoon, Sabby's mom gave him a lift. She would lie on her back and put her arm around him like a seat belt, pulling him up out of the water and onto her chest. She would swim for both of them, zooming him safely wherever they went.

When he was riding on top of her, he could look around like a sea captain high up on top of the ship.

As she taught Sabby how to swim and to dive, she also taught him to be very careful when he was near the shore, or any rocks or other dangerous places where he might get hurt.

. . . *And one of the places she taught him about was the Great Big Pipe.*

The lagoon and the ocean were connected by a long, metal pipe. (The fancy name is a culvert.) The culvert went beneath a wide land bridge with an old road people had built between the lagoon and the ocean.

People had also put big, jagged rocks near both open ends of that pipe to keep the road from crumbling. They did not think about how what they did might hurt sea otters.

Along the road, a sign on a white wooden fence said "**Danger: Swift Current! Stay Back!**"

Sometimes Sabby's mom would take him into the farthest corners of the lagoon, away from the surf and foam near the pipe, to visit with other otters, and to rest, play, or eat.

As you may have already guessed, to get to the lagoon from the ocean, they had to swim through the pipe. And they had to go through when it was full of noisy, foaming water rushing at high speed, which is hardly an easy task. That pipe was longer than a school bus—nearly fifty feet— and about as big around as a refrigerator.

Before making the journey through the pipe, Sabby's mom would patiently wait with him on her chest and make sure he understood what her plan was. Then she would open her mouth wide and grab his fine, thick fur with her teeth.

Just like a mama cat with her kitten, she would hold Sabby by the scruff of his neck. She would pause for just an instant, rise up, take in a deep gulp of air—making sure he also took in a deep gulp of air—and push him down below the surface. She'd take a last look around, then dive under.

She would pull him through the pipe with her teeth, blazing the path as fast as her flippers and tail could make her go.

Sabby was usually j-u-u-u-s-t running out of air by the time they made it through. He was thrilled when they came up at the end of the pipe and popped up to the sparkling surface for a big breath of fresh air.

He was always grateful to see the bright blue sky once again. Sabby loved the smell of that air.

Whew! What a swim!

The day of Sabby's great adventure in the lagoon began calmly with only a gentle salt breeze blowing. The smell of kelp was strong in the air.

Another sea otter mom floated nearby with her pup. This pup was a little bit older than Sabby. They drifted lazily on their backs next to each other, eyes closed and faces dry, sleeping in the warm sun. Their whiskers were dry, too, with paws, flippers, and noses pointing skyward.

Sabby was curious, but he did not want to create a big **commotion** by disturbing these other otters. So he decided to explore the interesting, sharp rocks that were right near him, and near the Great Big Pipe.

That was probably a mistake.

The **tide** was going out, creating a current that drained the water out of the lagoon just like emptying a bathtub. Without noticing it, Sabby was gently being drawn by the rippling current toward the pipe's giant mouth and the nearby jagged rocks.

Sabby's mom knew it was dangerous for little Sabby to be near the mouth of the pipe. She kept a close eye on him to make sure he was safe. Each time she came up to the surface from diving for food, the first thing she did was to quickly focus her dark, shining eyes and search around to make sure he was all right.

Sometimes when she was down underwater, Sabby started to call out in his little pup's voice. He worried she might not come back, and he felt scared and a little bit lonely.

"Eeeeh, eeeeh, eeeeh," he would cry.

The minute he saw her nose and face break through the water's surface again he was happy. And she was happy to see him. She would roll over, smoothly swim to him, and put her arms around him in a big hug.

On the day of the great adventure, Sabby's mom came up from diving, looked around, and saw that Sabby was very close to the Great Big Pipe. She feared he might be grabbed up by the powerful currents and sucked into the dark mouth of the pipe.

She swam right over to Sabby and took him by the fur of his neck and gently dragged him a safe distance away from those big, jagged rocks. Then she let him go and went back to diving for their lunch. It takes a lot of clams and mussels to feed two otters!

But yet again, Sabby poked his way over toward the deadly rocks. Sometimes his curiosity just got the best of him and he didn't pay close attention to where he was. He was a little stubborn that way. This time he was right at the mouth of the Great Big Pipe with the current now rushing through, tugging at him with more and more force. His mom was still underwater and couldn't see him.

When she came up and spied around for Sabby, she did not spot him. She began to worry and stopped everything else to look for him. She pulled herself high in the water to see as far as possible. She turned around in all directions, searching for Sabby.

She could not find him. To make sure he would know where she was, she began to cry out loudly, hoping he could hear her.

"Eeeeeeeeh! Eeeeeeeeh!"

But she got no response.

Now Sabby's mom got really worried. She called out even more loudly and spun around faster and faster to look in all directions. She swam to the right and swam to the left, keeping her head high out of the water so she could see. And she continued to call out to him.

She searched everywhere in the lagoon. What happened to Sabby? What happened to Sabby?

Then she spotted it: a dangerous **whirlpool** had formed at the mouth of the pipe.

Oh, no, Sabby had been sucked into the Great Big Pipe!

Sabby was in trouble. The current pulled him through the pipe. He had not taken a deep breath before being yanked under the surface and really needed more air. He was roughly tumbled, twisted, and spun. The sharp shells that lined the pipe scraped him.

It was dark and cold inside the pipe. He did not know where he was, where he was going, or what was going to happen to him. He did not know if he'd make it out.

Suddenly, his powerful natural instincts took over—those are the forces that guide us to survive, without thinking, based on who we are. Because he was a sea otter, the water was his home and his strength. He calmed down. He showed a new courage and began to move as only a sea otter can.

Sabby now understood. The best way to live is not to fight against the ocean and to always respect its power.

Sabby was young and determined. This new spirit helped guide him to safety.

Sabby was finally spit out at the other end of the pipe into the ocean. He shot up toward the surface and popped into the air and into the sunshine. He was all turned around and gasping for breath, with fur and tail flying. But he had made it through the pipe on his own!

He was thrilled to hear his mother calling out to him. But then he began to panic. Her voice was distant. Even though he could hear her, he couldn't see her, and he couldn't figure out where she was.

He cried out to answer her as loudly as his little voice could go. "Eeeeeh! Eeeeeeeh!"

Right away, Sabby's mom heard him crying out to her. Hooray!

But his voice was so far away, and she was puzzled. She could not see him, or smell him, or figure out where he was. At that moment, she was not sure if she was on one side of the land bridge and he on the other. They might be separated by the Great Big Pipe.

She wanted to rush through the pipe to search for him, but she knew she would not be able to hear his voice while she was underwater. This made her even more afraid—if she could not hear his voice, then she might lose him. Forever. What if she went all the way through and he wasn't there? Then what?

Sabby's mom sprang into action to do the only thing that might work. She was very smart.

She headed straight for the sharp rocks next to the pipe, still calling out so he might hear her. Then, rushing with all her might, instead of going through the pipe, she climbed out of the water onto the rocks.

Crossing the jagged rocks was difficult and dangerous. But that didn't slow her down. She raced up the cliff and across the grass like she was being lifted by a magical force.

She hop-walked to the road as fast as she could with her flippers and paws, which are much better for swimming and diving than they are for climbing up sharp rocks and crossing roads, especially in a great hurry. She made it up onto the edge of the road, and across.

She shot under the white fence on the other side of the road, now on the grass again.

She could still hear Sabby. She rushed and stumbled and tumbled but did not stop. Now she saw him!

Without slowing or stopping, she uncurled her body one last time and shot off the sharp rocks, diving into the water. She raced to him in just seconds.

Once she reached him, she grabbed him tightly with both arms and pulled him up to her chest as she rolled onto her back. She squeezed him. They looked into each other's eyes, overjoyed, and cooed with relief and happiness.

You'd swear you could see big smiles on both their faces.

With Sabby riding up on top of his mom once again, they zoomed into the safety of the Pacific Ocean. Breathing easier, with bright eyes shimmering, they finally started to play, twisting around each other up and down . . . a jumble of paws, flippers, noses, and tails, splashing in the foam.

Two whole weeks passed, and Sabby was swimming a little bit better every day. He was now more prepared to live a healthy life exploring the ocean and making his contribution to the world of all creatures.

He and his mom decided he was ready to go back into the lagoon.

On a crystal-clear day, with the bright sun high above, they swam in from the ocean waves toward the lagoon. The air was once again filled with the smell of kelp and the sounds of gulls. They headed steadily and surely through the rippling current toward the pipe's opening.

When they reached the spot, Sabby and his mom looked at each other. They each took a deep breath.

Together, they dove down into the sparkling water and once again went into—and through—the Great Big Pipe.

Once they came out on the other side, with the Great Big Pipe safely behind them, and a lifetime of other great adventures to come, they lived happily ever after . . . a jumble of paws, flippers, noses, and tails.

The End

— AUTHOR'S NOTE —

The first time I saw a sea otter, I was smitten. Though I was only a teenager at the time, I knew this dazzling little creature was endangered. But I only learned the full story many years later when I went all in, spending thousands of hours studying, observing, and photographing southern sea otters in the wild.

The story of the sea otter, like the story of our great ocean, remains unfinished. I came to understand how humans caused the near extinction of the sea otter. I began to see how we are repeating some of the same reckless behaviors that endanger the sea otter and other creatures and ecosystems with equally deadly consequences.

Today, fewer than 3,200 southern sea otters survive from the many thousands that once thrived along the California shoreline.

Sabby's story arises in this context. For two centuries, sea otters were commercially hunted for their luxurious fur. As a result, by the early 1900s this once abundant creature had nearly vanished from the Pacific Ocean. Researchers believed sea otters were extinct.

At that time, known only to a handful of people, *one tiny colony of around forty southern sea otters survived in the surf and kelp off a remote stretch of the central California coast near Big Sur*. In this isolated environment the uniquely resilient sea otter began to mount a slow, nearly miraculous comeback.

During much of the twentieth century, the southern sea otter population grew from this small, hearty group. In recent years, however, their recovery has been inconsistent. The population has now stalled at around 3,200, not enough to assure their continued existence as a healthy and sustainable species. Despite some hard-fought conservation successes, protection under the Endangered Species Act and other wildlife conservation programs, much more work needs to be done.

Human activities directly affect sea otters, as they are threatened by the impacts of climate change and accelerating sea level rise, pollution and oil spills, limited food supply, and disease. Some sea otters are illegally shot and killed each year, even though they are legally protected. Wildlife predation also takes its toll.

Sabby is resourceful and strong. But he and the other descendants of this once thriving species are extremely vulnerable. They depend on us because we have such an outsized impact on their ecosystem. In short, their environment is our environment.

The sea otter story fascinates me because it is both inspiring and a cautionary tale: the threats they face and the threats we face are mostly one and the same. Our good stewardship of the ocean — the impact of citizen action — will make the difference between life and death, not just for this little sea otter.

If this sounds like a call to action, it is: for children, young adults, and adults of all ages. Destructive habits are hard to reverse and will require that we commit to changing the relationship we have with our ocean and our planet. Whether sea otter or human, our futures are not guaranteed. The solution starts with each of us.

Kim Steinhardt, May 2019
Monterey Bay, California

Sabby the Sea Otter: A Pup's True Adventure and Triumph

Published by Craven Street Books,
an imprint of Linden Publishing.
2006 South Mary, Fresno, California 93721
559-233-6633 / 800-345-4447
CravenStreetBooks.com

Craven Street Books and Colophon are trademarks
of Linden Publishing, Inc.

ISBN 978-1-61035-353-3

First printing
Printed in China on acid-free paper.

Library of Congress Cataloging-in-Publication Data on file

Book design: Carla Green, Clarity Designworks

NOTE: The author took all photographs in this book with telephoto lenses in order to to maintain a safe distance and avoid disturbing the sea otters and other marine life.

— DEDICATION —

It would be easy to dedicate this story to Sabby and the great family of sea otters who are the subjects of this tale. But that would be to overlook the many dangers they face, and the fact that their very survival is currently threatened. So I'll also dedicate this book to the growing number of people of all ages who are taking steps in their daily lives to help save the great ocean so that all the creatures who depend on it can survive and flourish. These creatures include little sea otters—and people too.

— ACKNOWLEDGMENTS —

Bringing Sabby's story from the murky ocean waters to the sparkling pages of this book was only possible because of the enduring support and inspiration of my wife Madelyn, my sister Barbara, my brother Jeffrey, and my niece Rachel. For that, I am deeply grateful. I also want to thank Kent Sorsky and the other talented folks at Craven Street Books for making this project so enjoyable.

— ABOUT THE AUTHOR —

Kim Steinhardt is a writer and award-winning marine wildlife photographer whose stories and photos interpret the natural world for all ages and audiences. He has been an adviser and photo contributor to *National Geographic Kids* Explore My World series, and his work appears in other publications and on TV. In 2017, Steinhardt co-authored *The Edge: The Pressured Past and Precarious Future of California's Coast,* and he frequently writes and presents regarding sea otters, coastal advocacy, and the often-troubled relationship between humans and nature. He also serves as president of the board of directors of the Seymour Marine Discovery Center at the University of California at Santa Cruz.

I hope you have enjoyed this story, and I'd love to hear from you. Please visit **kimsteinhardt.com** or email me directly at **SeaOtterAdventures@gmail.com**.

— GLOSSARY —

Clam - A sea animal (shellfish) that lives in sand or mud at the ocean. A clam has two shells that clamp shut and protect its soft body inside.

Commotion - Disturbing actions or noise that may be surprising or confusing, like unexpected motion or shouting.

Current - A flow of water that is moving one way or another, sometimes slowly, sometimes very quickly.

Egret - A large white or beige water bird with a long neck and long legs often found wading in shallow saltwater hunting for little fish.

Gull - A gray or white sea bird that is very common along the edge of the ocean and other bodies of water and can be very noisy.

Heron - A large gray or gray-blue water bird with a long neck and long legs often found wading in shallow saltwater hunting for little fish and crabs.

Kelp - A simple plant like seaweed that uses the sun to help it grow. Some long kelps can grow to create underwater forests that provide food and homes for many sea animals.

Lagoon - A body of water that is cut off from another body of water like the ocean by a bar of land or sand, or coral.

Mussel - A sea animal (shellfish) that attaches very tightly to rocks along the ocean shoreline. A mussel has two shells that clamp shut and protect its soft body inside.

Octopus - A sea animal with no backbone, it has a soft, bag-like body and eight strong arms with small suction cups. They have large eyes and can change the color of their skin to blend in and hide among rocks or shells.

Pelican - A large water bird with a long beak and a pouch-like bill that is used to scoop up fish.

Sardine - A small saltwater fish that travels in schools (groups).

Sea urchin - A sea animal with no backbone and a round shell covered with prickly spines on the outside that help protect it.

Seal, Sea lion - Sea mammals that use blubber (fat) to stay warm in chilly ocean waters and use flippers to swim and dive, sometimes barking, grunting, or growling loudly above water. Once hunted for their blubber and skin, they are protected today in the United States.

Southern sea otter - A sea mammal that lives in the chilly ocean and uses very thick fur to stay warm. Once hunted for their fur, sea otters are now protected in the United States. Only about 3,200 southern sea otters remain alive today.

Tide - The rise and fall of the ocean as it changes each day back and forth between a higher level and a lower level.

Whirlpool - A powerful circle of swirling water that can pull things to its center, created when water flows come together from different directions.

— SEA OTTER FUN FACTS —

Did you know that sea otter pups don't know how to swim when they are born? That's why their moms must teach them how when they are very young!

Did you know that sea otters can keep warm even in the chilly ocean? Since they don't have any blubber to keep them warm (like seals, whales, and dolphins do), they must have very thick fur. They need as many as a million very fine hairs in each square inch of their fur! That means they have the densest fur of any creature on our planet.

Did you know that sea otters eat as much as a third of their body weight every day?

Did you know that sea otters sometimes look underwater for food but come up with trash that people throw into the ocean, like broken glass bottles or old rusted cans? This junk can hurt little sea otters!

Did you know that today only about 3,200 southern sea otters remain in the ocean? There were many thousands more before they were hunted until nearly none were left. We need to make sure they are safe and healthy and we don't do anything to create problems for them—like throwing trash into the water, or chasing and scaring them.

For additional information and resources, please check out kimsteinhardt.com.